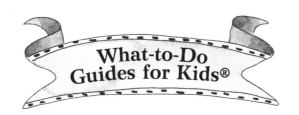

What-to-Do Guides for Kids®

What to Do When You
DREAD
YOUR BED

A Kid's Guide
to Overcoming
Problems with Sleep

by Dawn Huebner, Ph.D.

illustrated by Bonnie Matthews

MAGINATION PRESS • WASHINGTON, D.C.

To Darcie Johnston, for working your magic on this book
and so many others. I couldn't have conjured a better editor. — DH

Published by
MAGINATION PRESS
An Educational Publishing Foundation Book
American Psychological Association
750 First Street, NE
Washington, DC 20002

For more information about our books, including a complete catalog, please write to us,
call 1-800-374-2721, or visit our website at www.maginationpress.com.

Printed by Worzalla, Stevens Point, Wisconsin

Library of Congress Cataloging-in-Publication Data

Huebner, Dawn.
What to do when you dread your bed : a kid's guide to overcoming problems with sleep /
by Dawn Huebner ; illustrated by Bonnie Matthews.
p. cm. — (What-to-do guides for kids)
Summary: "Teaches school-age children cognitive-behavioral techniques to treat problems
with bedtime and sleep. Includes introduction for parents"—Provided by publisher.
ISBN-13: 978-1-4338-0318-5 (pbk. : alk. paper)
ISBN-10: 1-4338-0318-6 (pbk. : alk. paper)
1. Sleep disorders in children—Treatment—Juvenile literature.
2. Children—Sleep—Juvenile literature. 3. Cognitive therapy for children—Juvenile literature.
I. Matthews, Bonnie, ill. II. Title. III. Series.
RJ506.S55H84 2008
618.92'8498—dc22   2007039550

Manufactured in the United States of America
10 9 8 7 6 5 4 3

CONTENTS

Introduction to Parents and Caregivers

"**G**ood-night. Sleep tight. I love you." We all have this image: Of whispering our final, loving words to our children and tiptoeing out of their rooms. Of finishing the dishes or turning on the TV and finally, finally having a moment to ourselves as our children drift off to sleep.

But in many households, it doesn't go that way at all. Instead, bedtime becomes battle time. We fight about when. We fight about where. We fight about who's going to put them to bed and how many stories and whether or not to allow one more hug, just one more, please. We fight until we're exhausted, and they're exhausted, and no one is asleep. And then we give in. And we lie down in beds that are too narrow, or we take them into beds that used to be ours,

and we fall asleep and so do they. Eventually. But not the way we wanted.

One of three children has trouble falling asleep, impacting on just about everything else in their lives, from their mood the next day to their ability to focus at school. Sleep-deprived children are more vulnerable to a host of problems, from anxiety to uncontrolled rage to physical illness. And sleep-deprived parents don't do so well either.

There are many reasons why kids have trouble at night, why they (and we) don't get enough sleep. Nighttime fears top the list, followed by competing demands (homework, TV, too little family time) and the inability to settle down at night. Bad habits are quick to form yet seemingly impossible to break. And being short on sleep leads to physiological changes that actually make it harder to fall asleep the next night, creating a downward spiral of nighttime problems.

You know all that. And you have undoubtedly tried everything you can think of to get your child to sleep in a reasonable way, at a reasonable time. But as you know, there is no crib to contain your determined 8-year-old, no logic to appease your frightened 11-year-old, no routine to fully settle down your restless 10-year-old. You, as a parent, play an important role in helping your child develop good sleep habits, but by the time your child is 6, 9, or 12 years old, you no longer have the ability to solve the problem on your own. You need your child's help. That's where this book comes in. *What to Do When You Dread Your Bed* gives kids the tools they need to conquer common bedtime problems, from fears to busy brains to restless bodies. You can best support your child in developing new sleep skills if you read this book on your own first. Then, commit yourself to maintaining a consistent bedtime, even on weekends. That can be a challenge for busy families. But getting enough sleep is an essential part of learning to fall asleep and stay asleep independently.

After you have reviewed it on your own, read the book together with your child, helping him or her to follow the steps exactly. There are new skills for your child to practice, and new rules for you to enforce. Some of the rules might require substantial changes in your family's routine (turning off the TV an hour before bedtime – yikes!). Some might be met with resistance from your child. But hang tough! No caving. No apologizing. No exceptions. Follow all of the recommendations until your child is falling asleep and staying asleep consistently and at the proper time. Once that is happening, you will be in a better position to decide where to allow some leeway.

Avoid the temptation to rush through this book. Work on just one or two chapters at a time. Understanding and mastering each step as it is presented gives children the foundation they need to move forward with greater success. Some children might want to read ahead, especially when they see that each chapter begins with a magic trick. Don't let them. Instead, use your child's desire to learn the next trick as an incentive to keep working. When kids master a step, they can move on. Kids who race through the book, or read all of the magic tricks first, aren't going to get as much out of the program. If you and your child are following the steps carefully, and your child is still

taking longer than an hour to fall asleep, is awake for long stretches in the middle of the night, or is getting fewer than eight hours of sleep per night, you may want to talk to your child's doctor or consult with a therapist.

Keep your child moving forward, one step at a time, projecting an air of confidence in his or her ability to succeed. Encourage your child to practice, practice, and practice some more, sticking with the tough steps until they become easier. Then celebrate progress and move on. Watch for incremental changes: fewer call-outs, falling asleep more rapidly, sleeping through the night more often than not. All of these are signs that the program is working.

And then, there will come a time when you are able to put your child to bed, whisper "I love you," and tiptoe out. Without dread. Without tears and call-backs. Without nighttime awakenings and little bodies slipping into bed next to yours. Your child will have learned skills that can be used over the course of a lifetime. Because really, this is about more than just sleep. It's about tackling fears. It's about relaxing bodies and quieting minds. It's about setting goals and achieving them.

And the extra time at night, it's a gift to you. Enjoy!

A Little Magic

Wouldn't it be great if you could climb into bed, snuggle under your covers, close your eyes, and fall asleep without any fuss or fear?

Without listening for noises or thinking about bad guys?

Without an extra drink, or an extra hug, or an extra trip to the bathroom?

Without feeling too hot, or having twitchy legs, or lying awake for hours with your eyes wide open, knowing you'll NEVER get to sleep?

hungry

worries

need to be
with parents

good stuff
on TV

thirsty

too much
to do

Draw yourself lying in bed.

Circle the things that make it hard for you to sleep.

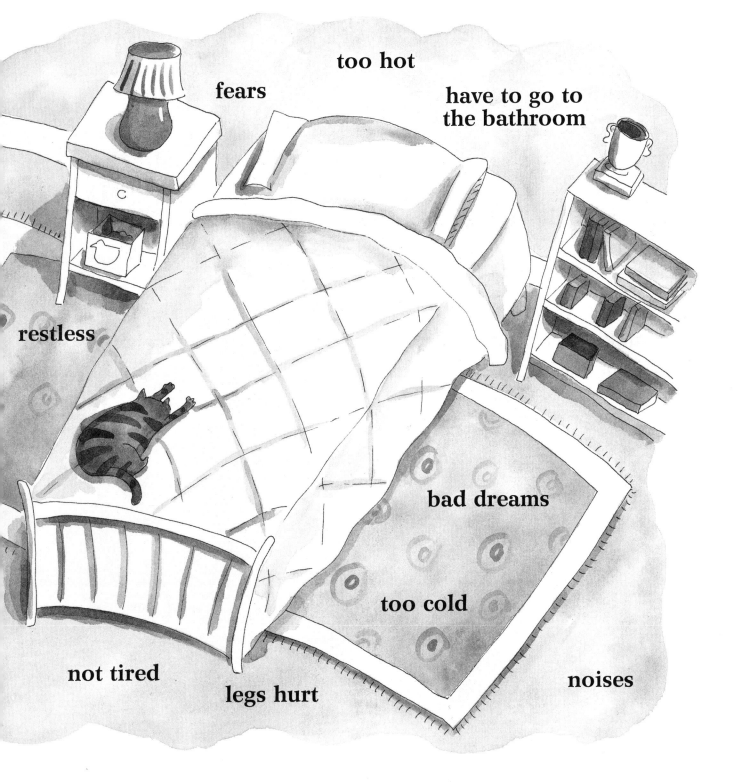

too hot

fears

have to go to
the bathroom

restless

bad dreams

too cold

not tired

legs hurt

noises

Maybe you're a kid who has had trouble sleeping for as long as you can remember. Or maybe your sleep troubles started more recently but aren't going away.

Maybe you feel scared when you get into bed, or you wake up in the middle of the night and need to be with someone to get back to sleep.

Maybe you can't settle down at bedtime because your body needs to be moving or your brain is too full of thoughts. Maybe you don't feel tired, or you are tired but you just can't sleep.

Maybe you think you're going to need a magic wand to make this problem go away. And maybe you're right. So let's create a magic wand.

Draw a magic wand.

What is a magic wand, anyway? It's just a stick of some sort, right? It can be a twig, a chopstick, a pencil, a drinking straw, or even your own finger. Anything long and narrow can be a wand.

But what about the magic part? Actually, anyone can create magic, because magic is really just a series of optical illusions. It's something that tricks your brain into seeing something different from what's really there.

So go find something you can use as a magic wand, and grab a rubber band. You're about to create some magic of your own.

The Jumping Rubber Band

1 Hold your right hand up, with your palm toward your face.

2 Place a rubber band around your ring finger and pinky.

3 Curl all of your fingers (but not your thumb) in toward your palm.

4 Stretch the rubber band around just the tips of your index finger, middle finger, ring finger, and pinky. The rubber band will now be tight against the back of your ring finger and pinky.

5 Keep your right hand curled in while you pick up your wand with your left hand. Wave the wand over your right hand, and say some magic-sounding words.

6 Let your right hand spring open. Watch the rubber band jump from your ring finger and pinky, where it started out, to your index and middle fingers. Magic!

Practice a bunch of times until you can quickly tuck your fingers and make the rubber band "jump" every time.

So you see, magic is about learning a bunch of steps, and then practicing over and over until you can do all of them smoothly.

Falling asleep is like that, too. Just a bunch of steps you do in a certain order and then—**VOILA!**—you're asleep.

You might be thinking, "A bunch of steps? All you have to do is close your eyes!" But as you know, it isn't always that easy. In fact, it can be really hard.

One of every three children has some sort of sleep problem. That means that in your class at school, there are probably six or seven kids who have trouble at night. You can't tell who they are. But you can be sure that some kids you know still sleep with their mom or dad, or sleep alone but feel scared about it, or take hours to fall asleep, or wake up in the middle of the night with bad dreams.

So if you're reading this book because you have trouble sleeping, you're not alone. There are kids all over the country, and even all over the world, just like you.

And just like you, there are thousands of kids reading this book, and learning to fall asleep and stay asleep without a hitch. Because really, there's more to it than just closing your eyes. There are a bunch of steps, and each one is important.

Think about the rubber band trick. If you decided to skip one of the steps, like tucking all your fingertips in, the trick would be a dud. No matter how many times you practiced opening and closing your fist, the rubber band would always stay on the same two fingers. If you don't follow all of the steps, it simply doesn't work.

It's the same with falling asleep. You need to do all the steps, exactly as they are described, in order to make it work.

But then it will work. Because even a problem that seems huge, like feeling scared every night or not being able to get to sleep on your own, can be solved pretty easily once you know the right steps.

Anyone can do it. Even you.

Important Numbers

Are you ready to learn another trick? You'll need a deck of cards for this one.

This One Is It

1 Count out 21 cards, and put the rest away. Deal the 21 cards face-down into three small piles, 7 cards in each pile.

2 Ask someone from the audience to choose a pile by pointing to it.

3 Pick up the pile that was chosen. Fan out the cards for the audience.

4 Ask someone from the audience to choose a card. Tell the person not to touch or tell you the card. Say, "Remember your card."

5 Fold the fan into a pile again.

6 Keeping all cards face-down, place the pile that's in your hand on top of one of the other piles. Then place the remaining pile on top. Now you have one big pile again, with the chosen pile in the middle.

7 Turn over the whole pile so it is now face-up.

8 Deal out the cards face-up into three new piles of 7 cards each, dealing from left to right. Put down the first card, then the second card next to the first, then the third card next to the second. Start back at the first pile for the fourth card. Continue left to right, until you have dealt out all of the cards.

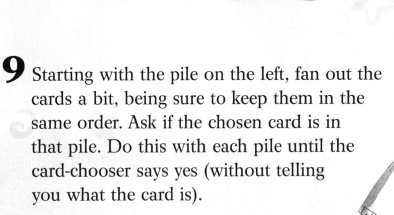

9 Starting with the pile on the left, fan out the cards a bit, being sure to keep them in the same order. Ask if the chosen card is in that pile. Do this with each pile until the card-chooser says yes (without telling you what the card is).

10 Pick up the chosen pile and place it on top of one of the other piles. Place the third pile on top, with the chosen pile again in the middle. Now you are back to one pile of 21 cards, with all of the cards still face-up.

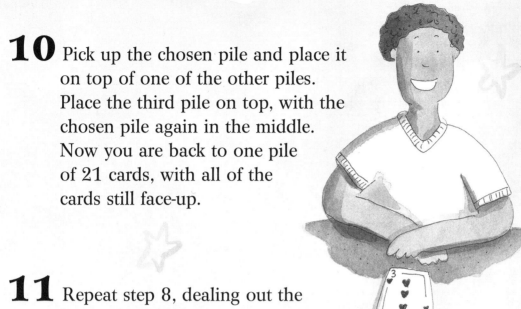

11 Repeat step 8, dealing out the cards face-up into three piles of 7 cards each.

12 Repeat step 9, asking which pile the card is in.

13 Repeat step 10, putting the pile with the chosen card between the other two piles, keeping all of the cards face-up. You have one pile of 21 cards again.

14 Turn the pile over so that it's face-down.

15 Use your best magician voice to announce, "Now I am going to find the chosen card!"

16 Say, "I am going to spell out 'This one is it' while I work my magic." Spell out T-H-I-S O-N-E I-S I-T, laying one card face-down for each letter as you say it.

17 When you get to the final "T" in the word "it," turn over *that card* to reveal the chosen one. Magic!

That trick is more complicated, isn't it? You have to get the numbers exactly right. If you start with 24 cards, or you deal the cards into four piles, it isn't going to work.

It turns out that getting the numbers right is an important part of sleeping well, too. Let's start with the number of hours of sleep you need. Kids in elementary and middle school need 9 to 11 hours of sleep. Not just on weekends, but every night. Check this chart to find how many hours of sleep kids your age usually need to feel their best.

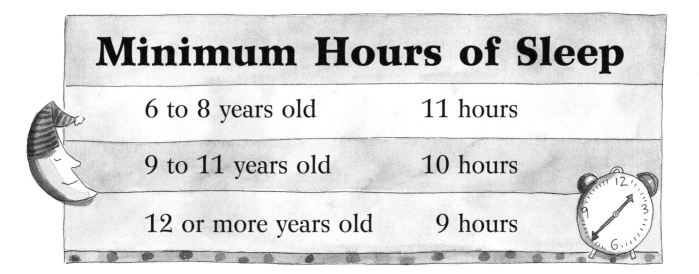

Minimum Hours of Sleep

6 to 8 years old	11 hours
9 to 11 years old	10 hours
12 or more years old	9 hours

These numbers are minimums, which means that most kids need at least this much sleep to get their brain and body work done and to wake up feeling good.

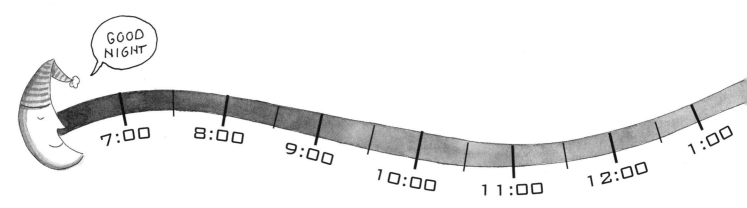

How many hours of sleep do you need to feel your best? If you aren't sure, check the chart or ask your parents what they think.

🌙 Write your number here.

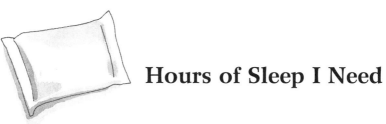

Hours of Sleep I Need

Now let's figure out how much sleep you're actually getting.

🌙 Using the timeline at the top of the page, circle the time you usually fall asleep on school nights.

🌙 Circle the time you need to wake up on school days.

🌙 Count the number of hours between the time you fall asleep and the time you wake up. This is the number of hours you are actually getting.

🌙 Write your number here.

Hours of Sleep I Get

Compare the numbers you wrote on the two pillows. If the second number is lower than the first number, you are not getting the sleep you need.

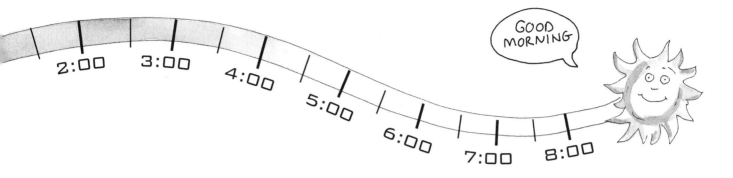

Interestingly, kids who don't get enough sleep often don't feel tired. And kids who are shortest on sleep sometimes lie in bed for hours, unable to get to sleep. It doesn't make sense, but that's the way it works. If you push past the time you really should be going to sleep, your brain shifts into a different gear, making you feel jazzed up or grouchy, instead of just plain sleepy.

And even though you may not feel tired, all kinds of things can begin to go WRONG. That's because while we're asleep, our bodies and brains are doing important things, things they can't do as well when we're awake.

Our bodies repair themselves while we sleep, healing cuts and fighting infections. Kids who don't get enough sleep get sick more easily and also take longer to get well.

We grow while we sleep—our fingernails and our hair and even our bones. When kids don't get enough sleep, their bodies get robbed of the sleep-hours they need to be healthy and strong.

Our brains are hard at work, too. While we're asleep, our brains sift through all the information we gathered during the day and figure out where that information needs to go. So if we don't get enough sleep, our brains are all a-jumble, making it hard to think and solve problems. Then little things start to bother us, and we feel tearful and cranky.

Sleep is actually one of the most important things we do. And we need to have enough of it. So the next two numbers to figure out are your best bedtime (the time you need to get into bed) and your best fall-asleep time (the time you need to be asleep).

GOOD NIGHT

7:00   8:00   9:00   10:00   11:00   12:00   1:00

🌙 Circle the time you wake up on school mornings.

🌙 Moving backward on the timeline, count the number of sleep-hours you need to wake up on your own feeling good. (This is the number that you wrote on the "Hours of Sleep I Need" pillow on page 20.) Put a square around the time. This is your best fall-asleep time.

🌙 Count backward from the square another half-hour. Circle the time. This is your best bedtime.

These are the first two numbers you need for your official Bedtime Plan.

🖋 Turn to the Bedtime Planner at the back of this book.

🖋 Cut along the dotted line, and use the Planner to mark your place while you are working through this book. That way, it will be nearby when you need to write something on it.

🖋 Write your name at the top of side 1.

🖋 Look at the timeline on side 1. Follow the directions to mark your best fall-asleep time and the best bedtime that goes with it on the timeline. Leave the rest of your Planner blank for now.

Is your best fall-asleep time the same as the time when you actually fall asleep? If so, you're all set in terms of time for now. But that's rare for kids who dread their bed.

Many kids go to bed at a reasonable time but lie awake for hours. If that's what happens to you, you're going to start your new Bedtime Plan by getting into bed later than you have been, half an hour before the time you have been falling asleep.

Let's say you get into bed at 8:30, but you don't fall asleep until 10:00. You're going to move your bedtime later, to 9:30, for a little while. Your bedtime will be at this later time just until you begin falling asleep more quickly. Then you and your parents will move your bedtime earlier, a bit at a time, until your bedtime and your fall-asleep time match the best times you wrote in your Bedtime Planner.

If you go to bed on time but lie awake for a long time, flip over your Bedtime Planner to the worksheet side and fill in part 1. This will help you figure out your new, temporary bedtime and how to gradually change it.

Some kids fall asleep quickly, but don't get enough sleep because they get into bed super-late. If this sounds like you, you're going to start your new Bedtime Plan by moving your bedtime 15 minutes earlier.

Let's say you get into bed at 9:30 and fall asleep right away, but really your bedtime should be 8:00. You'll begin by moving your bedtime up from 9:30 to 9:15. When you're falling asleep quickly at the new bedtime, you'll move your bedtime up another 15 minutes. You'll keep moving it up, just 15 minutes at a time, until your bedtime and fall-asleep times match the best times you wrote in your Bedtime Planner.

If you aren't getting enough sleep because you're going to bed too late, flip over your Bedtime Planner to the worksheet side and fill in part 2. This will help you figure out your new, temporary bedtime and how to change it.

All those clocks! All those times! It's a lot of numbers to keep track of, isn't it? But your Bedtime Planner will help. And as you inch your bedtime forward, you'll eventually circle a new bedtime that matches your best bedtime. And then you can say:

The Set-Up

Some tricks need preparation. For this next trick, you'll need a piece of paper, scissors, and two paper clips.

Link Up

THE PREPARATION:

1 Cut across the top of the paper to make a long, thin strip.

2 Fold the left side of the paper across the front of the strip, as if you're going to fold the paper in thirds.

3 Take one of the paper clips and join the two parts of the folded strip together, with the paper clip somewhere near the center of the folded part.

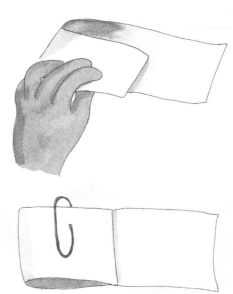

4 Now fold the right side of the paper, the third that was left over, *behind* the loop you created.

5 Take your other paper clip and join the new loop you just made to the middle third of the paper. Fasten the new paper clip to the left of the first paper clip, making sure you're clipping the right end of the paper to the middle only. Each paper clip should be holding two parts of the paper together, not all three parts.

6 Hold the two loose ends of the strip, one in each hand.

THE TRICK:

7 Show the audience that the paper clips are on two different parts of the paper, completely separate from one another. Tell them you're going to make the paper clips link together without even touching them.

8 Pull the two loose ends of the strip. The paper clips will go flying off and—**VOILA!**—they will be linked together. It works whether you pull the loose ends fast or slow. Experiment to see which way you like best.

POP!

ZING!

You are becoming quite a magician! It feels good, doesn't it? Part of being a magician, as you have seen, is learning how to set things up.

There's a set-up that works best for sleep, too. It has two main parts, a nighttime activity and a bedtime pattern. We'll talk about the nighttime activity first.

The nighttime activity begins half an hour before the best bedtime you wrote on side 1 of your Bedtime Planner. That means it starts a full hour before the time you need to fall asleep.

Your nighttime activity signals your brain that it's time to start winding down. When your brain gets this message, it tells your body to produce something called melatonin. Melatonin helps you fall asleep and stay asleep all through the night.

Our bodies produce melatonin when the lights are low. Nature helps by darkening the sky at night, making it easier for us to produce the melatonin we need to get to sleep. Of course, electricity makes things a bit more complicated, because when it starts to get dark outside, most of us turn on the lights. This confuses our bodies into thinking it's still daytime, so they don't produce nighttime levels of melatonin.

Keeping the lights turned down at night, which was nature's plan to begin with, helps our bodies stay on track. So beginning with your nighttime activity, it's best to stay in rooms that are dimly lit and to do things that are peaceful and relaxing.

Electronics (TV, computers, game systems) are not peaceful and relaxing. They're full of lights and sounds that make your brain think it needs to stay **ALERT**. And when your brain is alert, it isn't producing melatonin and winding down for sleep.

This means that in the half-hour before bedtime, all screen-based electronics should be turned off, especially if you're a kid who lies in bed a long time, unable to fall asleep.

It's hard for some kids to turn off their TVs and game systems. Try it for at least a few weeks to see if it helps you get to sleep. In the meantime, use your imagination to think of nighttime activities that are interesting and fun.

YOU CAN...

Go outside and look at the stars.

Play a board game.

Work on a puzzle.

Take a bath.

Draw a picture.

Read a book.

Follow the directions to mark the time for your nighttime activity in your Bedtime Planner.

Write down two ideas (not electronics!) for what to do.

You can do a different nighttime activity every night, as long as each one is relaxing and fun. So be creative. And when you're ready, read on.

Patterns

The next part of your set-up for sleep involves creating a pattern. But first a trick, right?

This trick is like the Jumping Rubber Band trick you learned in the first chapter, only better. This time you'll need two rubber bands. If you can find two different colors, that would be great. If the rubber bands are the same color, that's okay, too.

The Even-More-Amazing Jumping Rubber Band

1 Hold your right hand up, with your palm toward your face.

2 Place one of the rubber bands around your pinky and ring finger.

3 Take the second rubber band and loop it around your pinky. Make a twist in the rubber band, then loop it around your ring finger. Make another twist in the rubber band and loop it around your middle finger. Then make one last twist and loop it around your index finger. When you're performing this trick for an audience, you will lightly tug on each twist to show people that the rubber band is on tight, with no space for anything to get through.

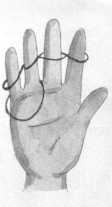

4 Just like in the trick you already know, curl your fingers (but not your thumb) in toward your palm.

5 Stretch the first rubber band so it goes around just the tips of your index finger, middle finger, ring finger, and pinky. That first rubber band will now be tight against the back of your pinky and ring finger. The second rubber band will still be twisted and looped around each finger, further up on your fingers.

6 Keep your right hand curled in while you pick up your magic wand with your left hand and wave it over your right hand, saying some magic-sounding words.

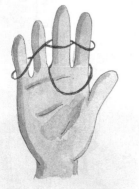

7 Let your right hand spring open. Watch the rubber band jump from your pinky and ring finger, where it started out, to your index and middle fingers, even though the twisted rubber band is still in place. Magic!

You know what's coming next, don't you? You're going to learn how the trick is connected to falling asleep.

It's a pattern. You turn to a new chapter. You learn a trick. Then you learn how the trick relates to sleep. You know what's about to happen, because it's been the same every time. When there's a pattern, you know what to expect and you're ready for it.

It's like that with sleep, too. (See!) If you create a pattern, your brain and body will know what to expect, so by the time you lie down and close your eyes—**POOF!**—you'll be ready for sleep.

Your bedtime pattern will begin just after your nighttime activity and end half an hour later, when you fall asleep. There are three parts to the bedtime pattern:

**Shift
Snug
Snooze**

Each part of the bedtime pattern leads to the next, so you can easily shift-snug-snooze your way toward sleep. If you look at the drawings below, you'll see that the time between the start of your nighttime activity and the end of your bedtime pattern is one hour. Here's how it works:

SHIFT

SNUG

SNOOZE

0 MINUTES

15 MINUTES

5 MINUTES

SHIFT

Your bedtime pattern starts with a shift activity to signal your brain that it's really and truly bedtime. Shift activities take less than 10 minutes and end with getting into bed. Your shift activity might be sitting at the kitchen counter for

a light snack before brushing your teeth, or saying goodnight to your pets on your way to the bathroom. Your shift activity should be the same every night. It's the start of the pattern that ends with closing your eyes and falling asleep.

Draw or write
a good shift activity.

SNUG

Your snug activity is what you do once you get into bed to help you settle down for the night. Snug activities help you feel safe and cozy. You can snuggle in your bed alone, or cuddle with your mom or dad. Snug time takes about 15 minutes.

For many kids, the snug activity is reading or listening to a story. But it could be something different, like telling about your favorite part of the day or writing in a journal. Remember that snug time needs to be quiet and peaceful (no TV or electronics!) to help you get ready to sleep.

It's best to have the same snug activity every night, especially if it usually takes you a long time to fall asleep. Once falling asleep is going better, you can switch between two or three different snug activities. But for now, choose one and stick with it.

Draw or write a good snug activity.

SNOOZE

Your snooze activity is the thing that happens as you are finding your favorite position and closing your eyes. It can be a kiss goodnight, a gentle back rub, or a whispered "I love you" right before your mom or dad leaves the room. It should  be the same every night, since it's the final part of the pattern that tells your brain, "Okay, fall asleep now."

Draw or write a good snooze activity.

Add the details for your shift, snug, and snooze activities to your Bedtime Planner. Talk to your mom or dad first, to make sure the things you want to do are okay with them.

Starting tonight (or as soon as possible), follow the steps you've written in your Bedtime Planner. Follow the pattern every night, even on weekends. That means you do all four parts, in the same order, every night: nighttime activity, shift, snug, snooze. If you are working on side 2 of your Planner, moving your bedtime and fall-asleep time earlier, the time to begin your nighttime activity and bedtime will gradually change. But that's the only thing that will change. You'll still do all the parts of the pattern, always in the same order.

As you do the pattern over and over, you'll notice that you feel sleepy as soon as you climb into bed. Your brain is anticipating what comes next and is helping you feel tired, just like it should. Soon you'll be falling asleep like a pro.

When Fear Gets in the Way

Okay, now you have a pattern in place, so your brain and body know it's time for sleep. But if you're like many kids, there's something that gets in the way—a pesky, hard-to-get-rid-of something. That something is FEAR, especially fear of the dark and fear of being alone. You know you'll need magic to tackle this one.

You're in luck, because there happens to be some magic specially designed to make these fears vanish. Go get your wand. And if you can't find it, that's fine, because this magic is actually a game, and any small object will do.

The Famous Fear-Melting Super Hiding Game

THE BASICS:

Start out by playing the Famous Fear-Melting Super Hiding Game during the day, when your house is nice and bright. Choose a section of your house to play in, like the kitchen, family room, and bathroom, or maybe the whole downstairs. You can play with your mom, dad, sisters, or brothers. Anyone or everyone can play.

Have everyone except you wait in one room (called the waiting spot) while you go hide your wand (or any small object). Hide it somewhere good, not impossible but definitely tricky. Keep just a bit of the wand showing. Return to where your family is waiting. Stay in the waiting spot while someone goes off to find the hidden wand.

Next, switch so someone else is the hider and you are the finder. If several kids are playing, take turns being the hider and the finder. Send the finders off one by one to spot the wand, but have them leave it in place until everyone has had a chance to find it. Only one person should be walking around the house hiding or finding the wand. Everyone else waits in the waiting spot.

If it's too scary for you to walk around the house by yourself, have your family sing a song from the waiting spot, loud enough for you to hear. You'll know your family is nearby because you can hear them, and you'll be able to go off to find a super-good hiding spot on your own. Your family can sing while you're finding the wand, too. After a while, ask your parents to sing more quietly so that eventually you're hiding or hunting without being able to hear anyone's voice.

LEVEL 2 CHALLENGE:

When you're ready to make the game a bit more challenging, expand the play area. Make the waiting spot one of the rooms downstairs, and hide the wand upstairs. If you don't have an upstairs, use a larger section of your house.

LEVEL 3 CHALLENGE:

When you're ready for even more challenge, play the game at night. Start with all the lights on. When that gets too easy, turn off the lights, except the light in the waiting spot. Finders can turn each light on and off as they go from room to room.

LEVEL 4 CHALLENGE:

Finally, to make it really tricky, play in the dark with a flashlight, or with only nightlights or closet lights on.

Play the Famous Fear-Melting Super Hiding Game for 10 minutes every day, changing it around to keep it interesting and fun. Time each other, or give clues like a treasure hunt.

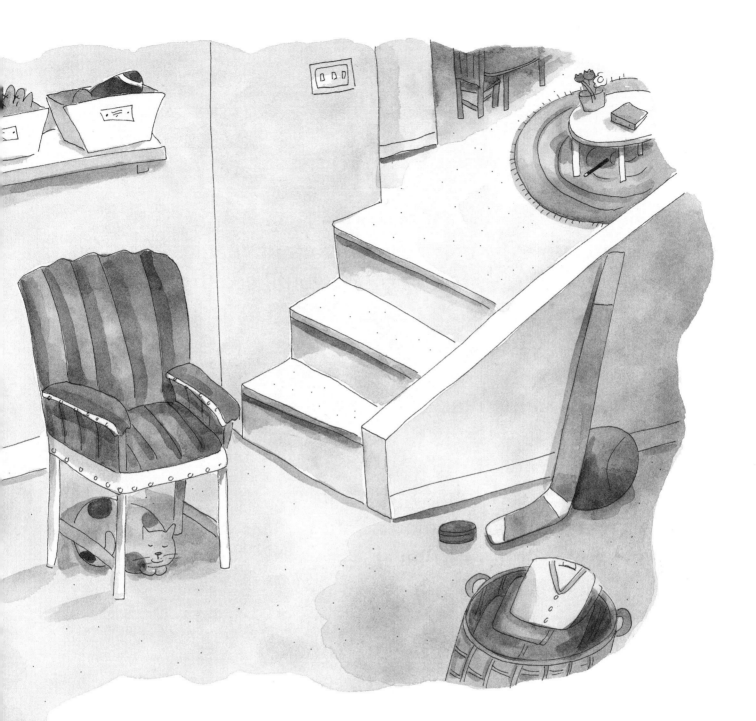

Work on stumping your parents. Become an expert finder. And let the magic work, game by game, to melt your fears away. Because after a few weeks of playing, you'll notice that being alone and being in the dark are totally okay for you.

ABRACADABRA! Those fears have vanished.

On Your Own

The more you play the Famous Fear-Melting Super Hiding Game, the more it will work its magic. After you have played for a week or more, you'll see that it's easier to spend long stretches of time in different parts of your house, totally on your own.

You'll be able to take the time you need to find the perfect hiding spot, or to search for the wand when someone else has hidden it. Even when you aren't playing the game, you will notice that it doesn't feel like such a big deal to be alone upstairs (or wherever your bedroom is). Which means it's time for the next step in your Bedtime Plan.

But first, a trick. Get ready. You are going to make a pencil move all by itself.

49

The Floating Pencil

1 With a pencil in your right hand, place your middle finger over the pencil and all other fingers behind it. Position the eraser end toward your pinky and the pencil's point toward your thumb.

2 Weave the fingers of your left hand through the fingers of your right hand, so all of your fingers are behind the pencil, except the middle finger of your right hand, which is holding the pencil in place.

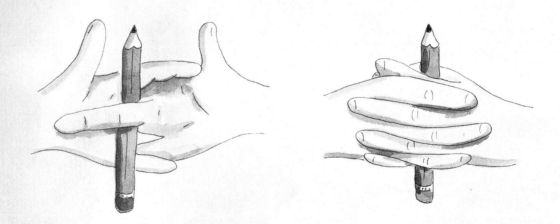

The pencil should extend beyond your hands at both ends. Make sure your fingers are tightly laced, so no one can see the hidden middle finger that is holding the pencil in place.

50

3 Rest the eraser end of the pencil on a table. Use your two thumbs to grip the top of the pencil, so it looks like your thumbs and the table are holding the pencil in place.

4 Tell your audience that you have the power to make the pencil float entirely on its own. Command the pencil, "Rise!" Lift your hands (and the pencil) up from the table and move your thumbs away, so it looks like the pencil is staying in place without anything holding it.

5 Slowly move your hands, still laced together, up and down and side to side. Tilt them a bit, backward and forward. (Be careful not to let the audience see the palm side of your hands.) Amazing! The pencil floats on its own! (At least it looks that way.)

6 When you are ready, shout, "Drop!" Quickly unlace your fingers and let the pencil drop to the floor.

Of course, the pencil wasn't exactly moving on its own. Your finger was holding it in place. (Don't tell!) Sometimes, something that looks like it's happening on its own really isn't.

Like falling asleep. You are probably falling asleep more quickly now. But you might not be falling asleep on your own. That's okay, because you've been working on two really important things—getting a bedtime routine going and getting to bed on time.

And now, it's time to begin doing it alone.

🌙 Find where you usually are on this list of falling-asleep-alone steps:

Step 1: Falling asleep in your parents' bed with your mom or dad.

Step 2: Falling asleep in your own bed with your mom or dad.

Step 3: Falling asleep in your own bed, with your mom or dad sitting across the room.

Step 4: Falling asleep with your mom or dad staying somewhere near your room.

Step 5: Falling asleep with your mom or dad anywhere in the house.

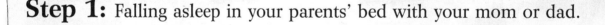

Starting tonight, move to the next step.

If you were at step 1, move to step 2. You and your mom or dad will now move to your room for your bedtime pattern and for sleep.

If you were at step 2, move to step 3. Your mom or dad will now move across your room and sit there after your snooze activity.

If you were at step 3, move to step 4. Your mom or dad will now leave your room entirely but stay nearby.

If you were at step 4, move to step 5. Your parents can now be anywhere they need to be while you are falling asleep.

Take a look at part 3 on the worksheet side of your Bedtime Planner. Put an X on the step you have been on. Then circle the next step, the step you will start tonight. Use your Planner to help you keep track of moving from step to step, until you are falling asleep on your own.

CLOSE YOUR EYES NOW.

At step 4 and step 5, your parents will leave your room, but they'll check on you every few minutes—just enough to peek in and whisper, "Close your eyes now," if you are still awake.

Some kids have trouble waiting for their parents, so they call out. Or they get up for a drink of water or to go to the bathroom. But really, they want to see their parents to make sure they are still nearby.

If you're calling your parents back to your room (or checking on them, wherever they are), you aren't truly falling asleep on your own. And you need to fall asleep on your own if you're going to get rid of your sleep problems once and for all.

So how about a game, to get rid of those call-backs and checks on your parents?

The Save-Em-Up Call-Back Game

THE BASICS:

To play this game, you need three call-back tickets. Make your tickets by writing CALL-BACK on three index cards or small pieces of paper.

Each ticket allows you to call your parents back to your room one time. If you call your mom or dad back, you use a ticket. If you get out of bed to find your mom or dad, that costs a ticket, too.

THE GAME:

Each night, tape your three tickets to your bedroom door before you go to bed. When you call out to your parents, they will come to your doorway and remind you in a calm, quiet voice that it's time for sleep.

SAVE-EM-UP CALL-BACK GAME!

CALL-BACK ▾

Then your mom or dad will take one ticket from your door.

Your parents won't answer your questions about tomorrow's lunch menu. They won't have a conversation about your birthday next April, or why Jamie is your best friend, or what happens during a solar eclipse. No repeat tuck-ins, no extra hugs or kisses. Just a gentle reminder: "It's time for sleep."

If you need to go to the bathroom or get a drink of water, you can do those things on your own. But if you see your mom or dad while you're up, **OOPS!** That will cost a ticket.

When you're out of tickets, you're out of call-backs. If you call your parents back or get up again, your parents will simply say, "No more call-backs." No matter what you ask or what you say, your parents' answer will always be the same.

You might get **ANGRY**, and you might start to cry. You might beg your parents for just one more hug, or suddenly remember something that seems really, really, really important. But your parents need to tell you, "No more call-backs," and stick with it. No matter what.

You might be thinking, "Hey, wait a minute, I thought this was a game! When does the fun part begin?" Well, here it is:

THE GAME:

Every morning, count the call-back tickets you have left. You get a point for each ticket you saved. When you have 10 points, you win. Then you get a prize, and the game starts over.

Each time you start a new round, talk to your parents about what your next prize will be. It could be something small from a store, like a package of temporary tattoos, or something fun to do, like bowling with a friend.

Think of three Save-Em-Up prizes you would like to earn.

Most kids say it's super-easy to win this game. Three call-backs is a lot, and besides, prizes are more fun than having your parents stand in your doorway to remind you that it's time for sleep. You might decide to save all your tickets to earn prizes. That's a prize every few days! Or earn prizes more slowly. It's up to you.

And in the meantime, keep reading. You're about to learn some brain magic to help you tackle the rest of your fears.

CHAPTER SEVEN

Bad Guys and Monsters

You've been working on your Bedtime Plan for a while now. You're probably falling asleep more quickly, closer to the right time, and more truly on your own. That's great! But if **SCARY** thoughts bump around in your brain, it might not feel so great to you. It might still feel pretty hard. Wouldn't it be nice if there was magic strong enough to overpower those scary thoughts?

Actually, there is. And you don't even need your wand to do it. It's brain magic, and you'll learn it in a moment. But first, we need to talk about chocolate ice cream.

Yes, that's right. Chocolate ice cream. (Hang in there. You know this is going to relate to magic in one way or another.)

Okay now, no matter what, DON'T think about chocolate ice cream. DON'T let an image of chocolate ice cream come into your mind. DON'T picture that mound of cold, wet, sweet chocolate right in front of you, ready for your spoon. Get chocolate ice cream OUT OF YOUR MIND.

Draw the picture that's in your head right now. And remember, DON'T THINK ABOUT CHOCOLATE ICE CREAM!

You thought about chocolate ice cream, didn't you?

It's almost impossible to NOT think of something. But now you know what you're supposed to NOT be doing, so let's try it again.

Read each sentence and draw the first thing that pops into your mind.

DON'T think about little mice.

DON'T think about your pencil.

DON'T think about fireworks.

DON'T think about monsters.

Wow, you aren't very cooperative, are you?

Actually, if you drew a little mouse, a pencil, some fireworks, and a monster, you're doing what everyone does. It's not a matter of cooperating, it's just the way our brains work. Even though we hear the DON'T part, our brains work so quickly that they've already found the "little mice" file and opened it up. Then the DON'T part registers, but it's too late. Our brains are already full of pictures of little mice!

It works better to tell ourselves, DO think of meatballs or jumping into a swimming pool or the last time we went skiing. That gives us something different to focus on, instead of trying to slam one file shut while not having another file to open in its place.

So what does this have to do with scary thoughts about things like bad guys and monsters? Well, you're not going to be able to simply NOT think them. It's like your brain is a giant TV. If a scary show is blaring, it's awfully hard to ignore. But there is something you can do. You can change the channel.

Decide ahead of time what you would rather watch on your brain TV. Make it something interesting and fun, like what you did on your favorite vacation, or what you want to do at your next birthday party. Then when the scary thoughts come on, remember that they are just a bunch of pictures. Change the channel.

What would you rather be watching on your brain TV?

Sometimes, though, scary thoughts are too strong. No matter how many times you try to change them, they keep coming back. When this happens, you can treat those scary thoughts like chewing gum.

That's right, chewing gum.

You know that when you first put a piece in your mouth, the flavor is super-strong.

Then you chew it and chew it and chew it some more.

Pretty soon the flavor is all chewed out. So you might as well throw the gum away.

Monster thoughts (or bad guy thoughts, or scary thoughts of any kind) are just like that. At first they're super-strong, so strong they frighten you. But you can learn to chew on those thoughts to make their scariness disappear.

The way to chew a thought is to think it. On purpose. A lot.

So if your scary thoughts are about MONSTERS, schedule a monster time at your house. Monster time should happen every day for at least 15 minutes, but not right before bed. You and one of your parents (and brothers and sisters, if they're interested) are going to use this special time to chew on monster thoughts. So get ready to be creative.

You might start by making up a funny song that has the word "monster" in it, and a dance to go with the song. Sing it and dance every day.

During a different monster time, write the word "monster" over and over, or type it into your computer using lots of fancy fonts to fill the page.

Pretend you're a monster, and have the rest of your family pretend, too. Make monster faces and use monster voices for a giant tickle fight.

Draw silly pictures of monsters.

The point is to write and speak and hear the word MONSTER again and again. You want to draw monsters and act like monsters and let your brain chew on monsters every day, until the scariness starts to fade.

Then shift to monster activities that seem more real to you. Draw the monster that frightens you. Have your mom or dad draw the worst monster they can think of. Then trade pictures and make them silly. Draw some sunglasses and a bathing suit on your dad's monster, and have him build a banana split on the head of yours.

Ask your mom or dad to print pictures of monsters from the computer. Take turns making up names for them. Tell spooky stories. Color realistic monster pictures, cut them into puzzle pieces, and put them back together again.

Keep thinking monster thoughts on purpose, in lots of different ways. Do it every day during monster time. And if monster thoughts come up at some other time, don't be too quick to spit them out. Instead, chomp on those monster thoughts. Think about your monster song. Remember what your brother looked like when he put his monster mask on upside down. Picture your mom's silliest monster picture.

Remember that these thoughts are just like gum. The more you chew them, the less powerful they will be. And after a while, you'll see that you can think about monsters (or bad guys, or any other scary thoughts you've been chewing on) without feeling scared. The flavor will be all worn out.

And when you don't want to be thinking about monsters, like when you're lying in bed at night, it will be easier to spit those thoughts out and switch to a different channel. It's brain magic.

PRESTO CHANGE-O

CHAPTER EIGHT

Busy Brains

Maybe you aren't scared at night, but your brain is brimming with other kinds of thoughts. If bedtime is the time you suddenly remember all the details from your day, it might be hard for you to close your eyes and fall asleep. There's too much to think about and tell.

If this sounds like you, it's going to be important for you to make time earlier in the day to talk about the things that come into your head at night.

Work with your mom or dad to schedule a daily talk time. It can be right after school, or just before dinner, or during your nighttime activity, but not any later than that.

Talk time is a time specifically set aside for you. It's a time to think about what's happening in your life, what you're wishing or wondering or worrying about.

Once you start having talk time, you'll stop having long conversations at bedtime. So when you're in bed and you suddenly remember, "Hey! The hamster in our class had babies today, and Vanessa pushed me at recess and she said she didn't even do it," your mom or dad will say, "We can talk about that during talk time tomorrow." This will help you get in the habit of asking your questions and telling your stories during talk time instead of when you're winding down for sleep.

Some kids' brains are so busy that even with talk time earlier in the day, they need something extra to quiet themselves down at night. One of the best ways to quiet your brain is to breathe in a certain way called circle breathing. Here's how it works:

Circle Breathing

1 Get comfortable and close your eyes.

2 Close your mouth, and take two slow breaths. In through your nose, and out through your nose. In through your nose, and out through your nose.

3 As you continue to breathe, imagine your breaths traveling in one nostril and out the other. In real life, you will be breathing in and out through both nostrils, but in your mind imagine the breath going into your right nostril and out your left nostril. Then reverse the pattern, and imagine the next breath coming into your left nostril and out your right nostril.

4 Imagine your breaths going in and out. First in through the right and out through the left. Then in through the left and out through the right.

5 In and out. In and out. Back and forth. Back and forth.

It takes concentration to picture the pattern. In through the right, out through the left. Then in through the left, out through the right. Keep it going, and you'll notice that when you concentrate, everything else fades into the background.

If your mind starts to wander and you find yourself thinking about your spelling test or the sleep-over on Saturday, just refocus your attention on your breathing. In right, out left. In left, out right.

Some kids fall asleep while they are circle breathing. Other kids use it to clear away the noise in their heads so they can relax and go to sleep.

Once your brain is quiet and you're breathing peacefully, your mind will start to wander. This feels good to some kids. They can just breathe and drift until they are asleep.

Other kids like to have something to think about while they're falling asleep. If you like to have something to think about, you can create a dream box.

Find a box and decorate it. Each night, you are going to pull something out of this dream box, so fill it up with dream ideas. Gather some of your favorite photos for your dream box. Cut pictures and words out of magazines. Draw things. Write the beginnings of stories. Fill your dream box with dream ideas that are creative, relaxing, and fun. (This would make a good nighttime activity.)

MAGAZINES

MARKERS

SCISSORS

GLITTER

A BOX!

TAPE

Here are a few ideas for your dream box. Add more of your own.

The time travel machine was finally done, so I stepped inside...

Dream Box

It was a magic garden. All I had to do...

Add to your dream box whenever you feel like it. Invite your mom or dad to add dream ideas, too. Then just before bed, reach into your dream box. Pull out a picture or the start of a story, something to think about while you're falling asleep.

And if you find your mind racing around, circle breathe for a few minutes to slow things back down. Then go back to your dream idea. Before you know it, you'll be sound asleep.

CHAPTER NINE

Relaxing Your Body

We've been paying a lot of attention to your brain, clearing away the fears and the jumble of thoughts that make it hard to sleep.

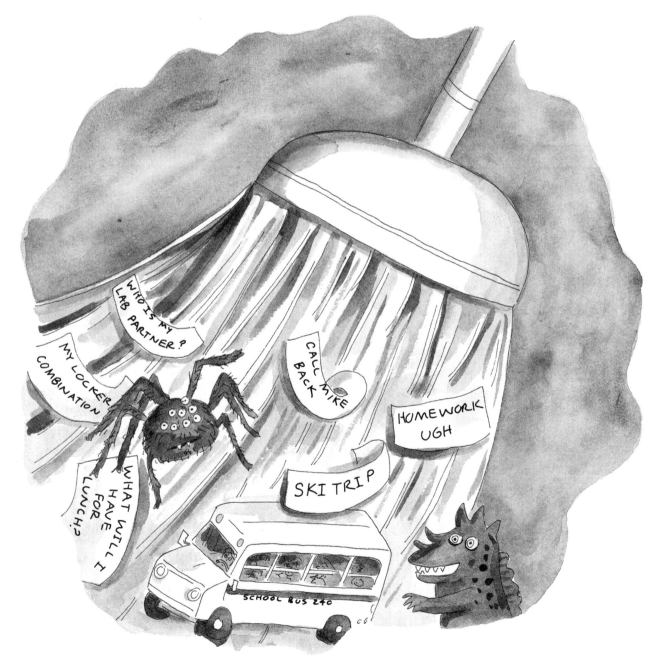

But sometimes it's your body, rather than your brain, that gives you trouble. Bodies can get twitchy and achy and uncomfortable, just when it's time for sleep.

If this is a problem for you, the first three things to pay attention to are food, exercise, and temperature.

FOOD

What you eat, and when, can make a big difference in how you feel. It's best to go to bed neither starving nor stuffed. For most kids, this means having a light snack shortly before bedtime.

A good bedtime snack might be yogurt, a piece of fruit, toast with peanut butter, or a small bowl of cereal. It should be something good for you, to help your body and brain do their nighttime work.

Make sure your snack doesn't have caffeine in it. Caffeine, which is in lots of sodas, coffee, and chocolate, keeps people AWAKE. Spicy foods and greasy foods are also not a good idea before bed.

Talk to your parents about foods you like that would make a good bedtime snack. Make a plan about eating something light and healthy to help you fall asleep.

EXERCISE

Have you ever noticed that when you have to sit still for a long time, like during an assembly or at the movies, you get the wiggles midway through?

If we don't get the activity we need, our bodies get restless and uncomfortable. Exercise during the day not only keeps us healthy and strong, it also helps us lie quietly in bed at night. Walking to school, playing tag at recess, going to baseball practice, and riding bikes in the driveway are all ways to get exercise during the day.

It's best to play sports and run around in the morning and afternoon, not too close to bedtime. The goal is to be active during the day, but gentle with your body at night.

TEMPERATURE

We sleep best when we're just a bit cool. It's almost impossible to get comfortable when you're too hot. And when you're too cold, shivering tightens up your muscles, making it hard to relax.

It's easy to take care of being too cold. Just put on warmer pajamas and socks, and throw an extra blanket on your bed.

It's harder to take care of being too hot. If the night air is cool, try opening your window. Fans help, too, and as an added bonus, you can focus on the gentle whirring sound. Taking a cool shower or bath right before bed lowers your body temperature. And you can sleep with only a sheet over you instead of your usual blankets. When you first get into bed, wave your sheet up and down a few times to create a cool breeze around you. Ahhhh!

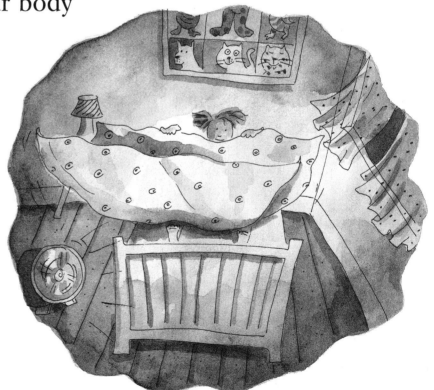

You're getting a nice, light snack. You're getting enough exercise during the day and not too much at night. The temperature is just right—not too warm, not too cold. But maybe you're still having trouble with **RESTLESS** feelings in your body. If so, there is something else you can do, right in your own bed, to help you settle down for sleep. It's called stretch-and-sink.

Stretch-and-sink teaches you to tense and relax your muscles. It's one of the best things you can do to get rid of that fidgety, gotta-be-moving feeling that bothers some kids at night. Here's how it works:

Stretch-and-Sink

1 Lie flat on your back, with your legs straight and your arms down at your sides.

2 Point the toes of your right foot, and stretch that leg as far as you possibly can toward the foot of your bed. Concentrate on making all the muscles in your leg *s-t-r-e-t-c-h* downward, as if that leg were growing longer than your other leg.

3 Count to 5 in your head.

4 Flex your foot, so that your toes are pointing up and back toward your head.

5 Count to 5 again.

6 Relax your right leg, and let it sink comfortably into the bed.

7 Now point the toes of your left foot and do the same thing, first stretching that leg as far as it can go toward the foot of the bed.

8 Count to 5.

9 Flex your toes, and count to 5 again.

10 Relax your left leg, so that both legs are sinking into the bed.

11 Now think about your right arm. Point your fingers, and *s-t-r-e-t-c-h* that arm toward the foot of your bed. Pretend there's a string pulling your arm down toward your feet.

12 When you can feel that pull, count to 5.

13 Relax your right arm, letting it sink comfortably into the bed.

14 Now point the fingers on your left arm, and imagine that string, pulling your arm down toward your toes.

15 Count to 5.

16 Relax your left arm, so that both arms are sinking into the bed.

17 Do five circle breaths.

18 If your body still feels restless, go through this whole routine again: Stretching and sinking. Stretching and sinking. Breathing, breathing, breathing.

When your body feels nice and drowsy, do some circle breathing and think of the idea you pulled from your dream box. Soon you'll be completely, restfully, happily asleep.

Nighttime
Awakenings

Kids sleep more soundly when they go to bed on time, follow a bedtime routine, and fall asleep alone. Going to bed in a healthy way actually helps kids sleep through the night. You might notice already that you don't wake up nearly as much as you used to.

You may still be waking up sometimes, though. Everyone does. We wake up just a bit, roll over, and fall back to sleep. If you wake up at night, that's what you can do.

Roll over.
Do a circle breath or two.
Think of your dream box idea.
Let yourself drift off to sleep.

But sometimes habits take over, and kids who are doing great at bedtime WANDER into their parents' room in the middle of the night. If this happens, your mom or dad will bring you back to your room and quietly remind you to go back to sleep.

If you're on step 3 of the falling-asleep-alone list and you're used to having a parent sit with you, your mom or dad will stay in your room as long as you're quietly falling asleep, just like they do at bedtime.

If you're on step 4 or 5, your mom or dad will leave your room and check on you again in a few minutes, just like at bedtime.

After a few nights of walking you back to your bed, your parents will walk as far as your doorway while you get into bed on your own. Then they will walk you as far as their doorway, so that little by little you'll be able to return to bed by yourself. With you and your parents all doing their part, you'll be amazed (like magic!) how quickly you'll be able to break the habit of getting up in the night. And everyone will get a better night's sleep.

CHAPTER ELEVEN

Scary Dreams

Everyone has nightmares once in a while. Most kids sleep right through them. Or sometimes they wake up, but only part way.

If you have a nightmare and are only partly awake, your mom or dad can come to your bedroom and sit with you for a few minutes. They can tell you that you're safe, that it's okay to go back to sleep. They can smooth your hair back from your forehead or hum softly. They can talk to you about the dream idea you pulled out of your dream box. If you are only partly awake, your parent's calm voice will be enough to help you fall back to sleep.

But if you're totally awake, the best thing to do is talk to your mom or dad about your bad dream. It might be tempting to try not to think about it, but you know how well that works. (DON'T think about chocolate ice cream. Ha!) It works better to think about the bad dream on purpose, to get your mind used to it (like gum, remember?), so you can spit it out and move on to something else.

Telling the nightmare, which is a way of thinking about it on purpose, takes away some of its power. And if you're awake enough, there's something more you can do.

Think about your dream as if it were a movie. Imagine yourself sitting in a big director's chair, and continue from where it left off. Only now, you're in charge. Give yourself special powers. Put in your favorite superhero. Make something funny happen, something totally ridiculous that makes you laugh.

If your nightmare is that dinosaurs are chasing you, put yourself back into the scene, with your heart pounding and the dinosaurs' hot breath on your neck. Then whirl around and shout, "You are extinct!" in your loudest voice, and watch the dinosaurs vanish. Or imagine getting swooped up by a miniature dragon with wings while the dinosaurs tumble over a cliff.

YOU ARE EXTINCT!

Learning to change your dreams is a powerful tool that gets easier with practice. If you're too tired in the middle of the night, do it the next day. Be creative. Be funny. It's your dream, so you can add whatever you want. Even though it's daytime and the nightmare is over, changing the end will help your brain learn how to shift more smoothly the next time you have a nightmare.

Think of a recent bad dream. Write it here.

Create a new ending that is powerful, magical, or silly, and that puts you back in charge.

CHAPTER TWELVE

Sleep Tight

Even though they look easy, magic tricks can be hard. You have to get all of the steps just right. And even when you're trying your best, things sometimes go wrong. It's FRUSTRATING when that happens. But magic tricks are fun, so if you're like most kids, you're probably willing to work at them without giving up.

It's the same with sleep tricks. Sometimes they're hard. They definitely require practice. But they're important, so don't give up. If one of the sleep tricks seems especially hard, read that section again and work on it until it gets easier. Then move on.

STRETCH

CIRCLE BREATH

CALL-BACK

CALL-BACK

And if you do, if you really work on all of the sleep tricks, you'll see that something quite amazing happens.

You'll learn to fall asleep. By yourself. In your own bed.

Without any fuss or fear.

Without listening for noises or thinking about bad guys.

Without an extra drink, or an extra hug, or an extra trip to the bathroom.

Without feeling too hot, or having twitchy legs, or lying awake for hours with your eyes wide open, knowing you'll never get to sleep.

Kids who go through the steps described in this book no longer DREAD their beds. They fall asleep quickly and wake up feeling great.

SO REMEMBER

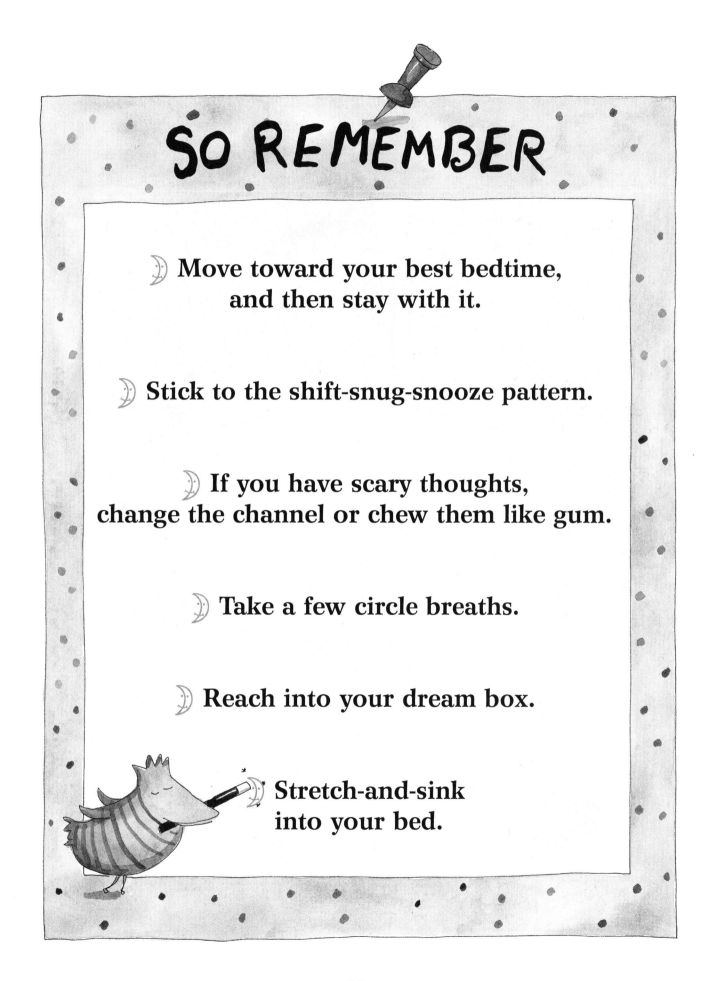

)) Move toward your best bedtime, and then stay with it.

)) Stick to the shift-snug-snooze pattern.

)) If you have scary thoughts, change the channel or chew them like gum.

)) Take a few circle breaths.

)) Reach into your dream box.

)) Stretch-and-sink into your bed.

Draw yourself sleeping soundly in your own bed.

It's going to feel so good!

BEDTIME PLANNER

FOR _____

T he Bedtime Planner is your guide to a good night's sleep. This side will help you work out the details of your personal bedtime plan. Side 2 will help you fix problems with getting to sleep on time and falling asleep alone. You will be filling out the Planner just a bit at a time, when and how the book tells you. And when your Planner is complete, you can put it near your bed to help you remember your plan. Sleep tight!

7:00 7:15 7:30 7:45 8:00 8:15 8:30 8:45 9:00 9:15 9:30 9:45 10:00

Find your BEST FALL-ASLEEP TIME on the timeline (see pages 22-23). Circle it.

Count 30 minutes back to your BEST BEDTIME. Put a square around it.

Count 30 minutes back to the time your NIGHTTIME ACTIVITY begins.
Put a triangle around it.

NIGHTTIME ACTIVITY

My nighttime activity begins at: _____ . My nighttime activity ideas are:

ONE IDEA	ANOTHER IDEA

BEST BEDTIME (30 minutes after nighttime activity begins)

My best bedtime is: _____ . My bedtime pattern ideas are:

SHIFT ACTIVITY	SNUG ACTIVITY	SNOOZE ACTIVITY

BEST FALL-ASLEEP TIME (30 minutes after best bedtime)

My best fall-asleep time is: _____ .

WORKSHEET

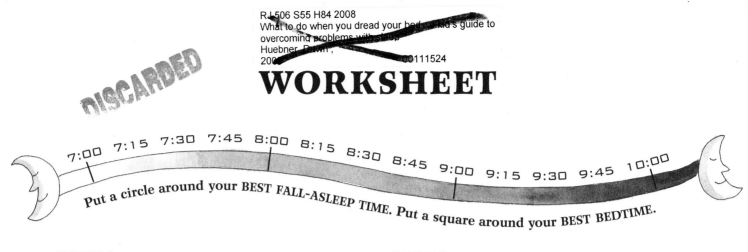

7:00 7:15 7:30 7:45 8:00 8:15 8:30 8:45 9:00 9:15 9:30 9:45 10:00

Put a circle around your BEST FALL-ASLEEP TIME. Put a square around your BEST BEDTIME.

PART 1

If you get to bed on time, but lie awake for a long time before falling asleep:

On the timeline below, put a big X on the time you have been falling asleep.

Count back two blocks of time (30 minutes) and circle that time. This is your new bedtime (for now).

Stick with this new bedtime until you have fallen asleep quickly four nights in a row.

Then move your bedtime up another 15 minutes. Cross out the old circle, and put a circle around your new bedtime. Stick with the new bedtime until you have fallen asleep quickly four nights in a row.

Keep moving your bedtime up 15 minutes at a time (crossing out the old time and circling the new one), until your bedtime and fall-asleep time match your best times at the top of this worksheet.

PART 2

If you get into bed later than your best bedtime, but fall asleep quickly:

On the timeline below, put a big X on the time you have been getting into bed.

Count back one block of time (15 minutes) and circle that time. This is your new bedtime (for now).

Stick with this new bedtime until you have fallen asleep quickly four nights in a row.

Then move your bedtime up another 15 minutes. Cross out the old circle, and put a circle around this new bedtime. Stick with the new bedtime until you have fallen asleep quickly four nights in a row.

Keep moving your bedtime up 15 minutes at a time (crossing out the old time and circling the new one), until your bedtime and fall-asleep time match your best times at the top of this worksheet.

7:00 7:15 7:30 7:45 8:00 8:15 8:30 8:45 9:00 9:15 9:30 9:45 10:00 10:15 10:30 10:45 11:00 11:15 11:30

PART 3

If you have trouble falling asleep alone:

In the list below, put an X on the step number you are currently on.

1: Falling asleep in your parents' bed with your mom or dad.
2: Falling asleep in your own bed with your mom or dad.
3: Falling asleep in your own bed, with your mom or dad sitting across the room.
4: Falling asleep with your mom or dad staying somewhere near your room.
5: Falling asleep with your mom or dad anywhere in the house.

Now circle the next number down. Starting tonight, this is the step you are on.

Stay at the new step until you have fallen asleep smoothly for one week.

Then move down to the next step by putting an X on the old number and circling the new number. Stay at the new step until you have fallen asleep smoothly for one week.

Keep moving down to the next step (crossing out the old number and circling the new one) until you are at step 5.

SIDE 2